PATTON:

Many Lives, Many Battles

General Patton and Reincarnation

Karl F. Hollenbach

ISBN: 1481257439
ISBN-13: 978-1481257435

First publication in Venture Inward magazine, September-October 1989, by the Association for Research and Enlightenment, 215 67th Street, Virginia Beach, VA 23451-2061, USA.

The article was re-published, with permission, in a Japanese anthology.

Second publication by Dunsinane Hill Press, P.O. Box 5184, Louisville, KY 40205, USA.

Third publication in 2012 by internet marketing, LLC, Louisville, KY, USA.

DEDICATION

Dedicated to General George S. Patton, Jr. –
A Military Genius.

CONTENTS

Lt. General George S. Patton, Jr.
at beachhead, Gela, Sicily, 11 July, 1943

ACKNOWLEDGMENTS -

Reprinted from Venture Inward magazine, September-October 1989, with kind permission of the Association for Research and Enlightenment, Inc., P.O. Box 595, Virginia-Beach, Virginia 23451.

Special thanks to A. Robert Smith, Editor.

Cover artwork by Karen Kluge-Waller, whose kind permission to use on the front cover was given to the author on November 28, 2012.

Art Direction/Design by Francis Sporer.

Special thanks to James Autenrith, who played the organ during the visitation and the funeral of General Patton, for adding his memories of one of history's greatest military leaders.

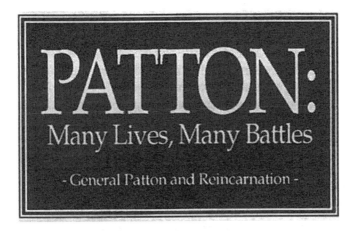

1 ORIGINAL PAMPHLET

General George S. Patton, Jr. believed in reincarnation and expected to serve his country again in a future life as a soldier. Admirers of Patton, who have difficulty with reincarnation as a theory, let alone as a fact, either rationalize Patton's belief in past lives or ignore it.

One biographer suggested that Patton's vast reading of military history allowed his imagination to visualize himself living in the time of Caesar or Napoleon. Another stated that when Patton said, "l have been on this battlefield before," he merely meant he had studied it.

Whether reincarnation is accepted or rejected as a fact, what is important, for an understanding of

General Patton, is that for him it was a fact, a personal experience, and a recollection.

Beneath his rough exterior, Patton was a compassionate, intelligent gentleman. While he could strut imperiously as a commander, he would also go down on his knees and pray upon receiving a momentous message.

While he was no politician, Patton did see things in their long and wide range. He thought he had a duty to perform for his country and always felt confident that he could do what he was told to do, without letting personal interest or danger interfere.

In November 1942, he wrote his wife, "When this job [the North African landing] is done, I presume I will be pointed to the next step in the ladder of duty. If I do my full duty, the rest will take care of itself." Some months later he wrote her that he felt like a "chip on the river of destiny" going to some predestined place which he did not know, but his chief concern was to do his duty while following his star. In his diary he wrote, "Duty is but discipline carried to its highest degree."

In *Patton: A Study in Command,* Major General Essame, who commanded a British infantry brigade in World War II, said that Patton brought an "exceptionally lively mind and vivid imagination" to the study of military history and stood with other great battlefield commanders as Murat, Sherman, Forrest, Stonewall Jackson, and Rommel.

A captured German officer, Lt. Col. Freiherr Von Wagenheim, said that Patton was the most feared general on all fronts, as well as being the most modern general and best commander of armored and infantry troops combined. Patton's intelligence officer said that most of the time Patton, "with his psychic seismograph," was far ahead of his "G-2" [intelligence]. Patton himself said that he had a sixth sense and could guess the intentions of the enemy better than a staff of G-2. Consequently, he preferred a loyal staff rather than a smart one.

At the close of World War II, Vincent Sheean in a radio broadcast said that Patton was the "most original, the boldest, and the most modem talent" in field operations that America had produced.

Patton was born November 11, 1885, on lands given to his parents by his maternal grandfather, a rancher of enormous holdings in the San Gabriel Valley of California. His father kept him home and read him the classics, believing that the usual curriculum of the public schools was an undue burden for a young mind. Consequently, when young George began his formal education at age 12, he could recite passages from the Iliad and the Bible by heart. He was influenced also by his father's study of C.A.L. Totten's book about predictions of the future based on the measurements of the Great Pyramid. Patton, who experienced "deja vu" and sometimes claimed the power of prophecy, felt certain in the late 1920s (when he was in his forties) that there would be another major war.

As a youth, Patton fancied himself to be King Arthur and would pull at an old bolt in a wall near the woodshed as though it were Excalibur. He also wore a wooden sword into which he had burned "Lieutenant General George S. Patton, Jr.," unaware at the time that there were full generals.

He did everything he could to become a soldier. In 1909, at age 24, he wrote the father of his childhood sweetheart (and future wife) Beatrice, that it was as natural for him to be a soldier as it was to breathe. He had told Beatrice that it was in war alone that he was fitted to be anything of importance.

Although he would have dreaded becoming a clergyman, the only thing that possibly could have prevented him becoming a soldier was "the call". He called himself a "communicant of the Episcopal Church" and said he attended service every Sunday.

A cavalry officer, Patton competed in five events in the 1912 Olympic Games in Stockholm. He served as an aide to General John J. Pershing during the punitive pursuit of Pancho Villa into Mexico in 1916. He continued as an aide to Pershing (who almost became Patton's brother-in-law) until he transferred to the new Armored branch as the first U.S. Commander of Armor.

In World War I in France, after his tank brigade took the Village of Varennes, he continued to attack on foot. Later he wrote that when he began to tremble with fear, he suddenly thought of his ancestors and seemed to see them in a cloud over the enemy lines in front of him. Instantly becoming calm, he said aloud, "It is time for another Patton to die." (His paternal grandfather had been killed in the Civil War.) Going forward to what he believed to be certain death, Patton was hit by machine-gun fire and suffered serious wounds. The following month, he wrote to his father that his "Guardian Spirits!" couldn't be blamed for one slip, as they must have had a difficult job keeping him from being killed.

Traveling in France before that war, Patton recognized with apparent foreknowledge that the countryside in which Henry I of England had taken possession of Mains in the 12th Century, would again become a battlefield. His report was filed and forgotten, until 1944 when the success of his drive as commanding general of the Third Army in World War II was facilitated, as he himself put it, by his personal reconnaissance 30 years before.

When Eisenhower was appointed Commander-in-Chief of all Allied Forces in North Africa, Patton wrote in his diary that he was proud of Eisenhower, but thought he (Patton) could do better in the same job; however, he felt that he lacked something that made politicians trust Eisenhower.

Patton's nephew wrote that those things that glowed in a romantic light or were tinged mystically were almost always the things that were very real for his uncle. A firm believer in the power of extrasensory perception (he probably wouldn't have called it that), Patton felt sure that the faculties of telepathy, deja vu, prophecy, and reincarnation were somehow parts of a whole, according to biographer Fred Ayer, Jr., in *Before the Color Fades*.

Considering these powers a gift, Patton believed that he was among the handful of men in the entire world who possessed them. All through his life, he said, every time he had become bitterly disappointed, things worked out for the best, proving to be a blessing in disguise, and finally working to his advantage, although he could not see it at the time. With mystic assurance, Patton accepted as fact that God predetermined everything good that happened to him. He felt certain that ancestors remain with us, he would fight once more for his country in this life and most certainly again in another incarnation.

When his nephew once asked him, "Do you really believe in reincarnation?" Patton answered, "I don't know about other people, but for myself there has never been any question. I just don't think it, but I know there are places that I've been before and not in this life."

He then told of his experience when he took his first command in France. A young French officer offered to show him around, but Patton said that was not necessary because he (Patton) knew the place well, Of course, the officer did not believe him, so Patton told their driver where to go in the small French city, almost as if someone were whispering the directions in his ear. Patton took him to what had been the Roman Amphitheater, the drill grounds, the Forum, the Temple of Mars and Apollo, and even showed him correctly the spot where Caesar had earlier pitched his tent. "But I never made a wrong turn," he said. "You see, I had been there before."

Even as a young man, he believed he would lead one of the two largest armies of the United States. Patton's nephew was able to meet with him for a short time during the Third Army's push across France. Patton told him that a man needed to know his own destiny; he must know what he was meant to be. Once or twice, he said, or at the most three times, Fate will reach out and tap a man on the shoulder, but usually the reply is, "Go away," or "I don't know you." But with imagination a man would turn around and fate would point out the direction. "If he has the guts," said Patton, "he will take it."

When Patton left for North Africa in 1942, he told his wife that he did not expect to return, his idea of glory being death on the battlefield. Patton did return, however, receiving a hero's welcome in Boston in June of 1945. Later, when preparing to return to occupation duty in Europe, he told his children that he would say goodbye, because he would never see them again. He expected to be buried on foreign soil.

When the children protested his gloomy prophecy, he cryptically replied, "It is true and has been revealed to me." He said he did not know how it was going to happen, but he was going to die in Europe and wanted to be buried there.

Patton returned to Europe where he was injured in an auto accident on December 9, 1945. His neck was broken, and he was paralyzed from the neck down

In the hospital, he told a nurse that all the attention given to him was a waste of taxpayers' money, because within a fortnight he was fated to die.

On December 21, Patton said several times, "I am going to die." By 6 p.m. that evening, General George S. Patton, Jr. passed over.

In his poem "Valor," he wrote: "Death is nothing... Valor is all."

APPENDIX A

In 1944 General George S. Patton, Jr. wrote a poem which he titled "Through A Glass, Darkly" as he and his third Army pushed through France into the Nazi Third Reich. Foreshadowing his role as Commander of a conquering army, Patton described previous lives he remembered as a combatant "in the dimness of the shadows" and in "later clearer vision" could sense, feel, hear and see battles he had fought in previous lives.

The poem consists of twenty-four, four-line stanzas with the rhyme being ABCB. In the first eight stanzas his "visions are not clear and he "cannot name" the battles, but he sees "the twisted faces" and feels "the rending spear." In his first reference to the role of a particular person, he writes that he may have "stabbed our Savior," while in other lives he has "called his name in blessing."

The next seven stanzas recount Patton's awareness of being a certain type of soldier at a particular battle. As a Greek Hoplite, he fights Cyrus, the Persian King, in the sixth century B.C., and he sees the Persian chariots turn in panic as the Greek phalanx extended their long spears.

The Classical Greek warrior–the Hoplite–carried a large round shield, an eight-foot spear, a short sword and wore a crested, bronze helmet and greaves. A Greek phalanx consisted of Hoplites formed in tight ranks. Ranging from eight to twelve ranks, the troops protected themselves with overlapping shields and attacked with leveled spears.

On his way to Egypt, Alexander the Great in 333 B.C. smashed the Persian army of Darius, securing the Persian naval bases except for the island of Tyre. In the following five-month siege, Patton as a Greek, seeing Tyre turned from an island into a peninsula by Alexander's engineers, reaches the walls of Tyre, hearing "the crash of tons of granite."

Patton, as a Roman Legionnaire, fights the Parthians with the Roman gladius, a short sword of 25 – 32 inches, in the first century B.C. He remembers suffering and finally dies from several arrows in his neck.

The Battle of Crecy, which took place in 1346, was the first important battle of the Hundred Years War. The English army under Edward III wiped out nearly half of the much larger French army, including over a thousand knights. As one of the French knights, Patton's armor was pierced by a lance that ripped through his entrails. Patton seemed to prefer being a French warrior, as will be seen in his last remembered soldier's role.

The following three stanzas relate lives fought on the seas. Patton recalls hearing the enemy bulwarks explode from point-blank round shot and sees bubbles rising after throwing captives overboard. Fighting with gun and cutlass, he feels Hell's flame within himself, as well as a rope around his neck.

Patton's predilection for being a French warrior occurs during the Napoleonic Wars, when, as a general, he "galloped with Murat." Prince Joachim Murat, King of Naples and French Marshal, was a flaunting cavalry commander under Napoleon I.

As commander of the newly formed United States tank unit during World War I, Patton describes his slow walk into enemy fire, where he received severe wounds. Returning to his permanent rank of Major, Patton returned to the cavalry until the beginning of World War II, when he became a Major General of a tank division. As a Lieutenant General, he led the Seventh Army in the invasion of Sicily and a year later, as commander of the Third Army, crossed France into Germany. Shortly after attaining the rank of a four star general, Patton died from an automobile accident and was buried in a U.S. Army cemetery in France.

He ends his poem seeing, as through a glass, darkly, the world's continuing strife, in which he fought "in many guises, many names."

He concludes that in the future he shall "battle as of yore, dying to be a fighter, but to die again, once more."

APPENDIX B

Commanders and Reincarnation

Prominent Americans who believed in reincarnation include: Ralph Waldo Emerson, Henry David Thoreau, Henry Wadsworth Longfellow, Walt Whitman, Edgar Allen Poe, Mark Twain (Samuel Longhorn Clemens), Henry Ford, George Vanderbilt and J. Paul Getty.

Benjamin Franklin wrote his epitaph at the age of twenty-two in almost a dozen different versions for his friends:

The Body of B. Franklin,
Printer,
Like the Cover of an Old Book,
Its Contents Torn Out
And
Stripped of its Lettering and Gilding,
Lies Here
Food for Worms,
But the Work shall not be Lost,
For it Will as He Believed
Appear Once More
In a New and a more Elegant Edition
Revised and Corrected
By the Author.

J. Paul Getty, the American oil billionaire, believed he was the reincarnation of Hadrian, Roman Emperor from 117 to 138 A.D.; Getty tried to emulate him and had his architect base the design for the first Getty museum in California on Hadrian's villa at Herculaneum. Hadrian's architects also built the Pantheon and Castel Sant'Angelo, which was originally built as a mausoleum for Hadrian and his dynasty.

Like Patton, other commanders of armies believed in reincarnation. Julian, nephew of Constantine the Great and himself Roman Emperor from 361 to 363 A.D., believed himself to be the reincarnation of Alexander the Great.

The Norwegian dramatist and poet, Henrik Ibsen, dwelt on this theme in his play "The Emperor and Galilean." Mortally wounded on the battlefield, Julian, as he lay dying entered into a metaphysical discussion concerning the nature of the soul with philosophers Piscus and Maximus. This illustrates, as with the death of Socrates, a philosophic calm, and utter fearlessness that comes from deep conviction in immortality.

Julian, an initiate into the Eleusinian mysteries, was a Neoplatonist, whose 18 months as Emperor was renowned for its enlightenment and religious tolerance. Exiled Christian Bishops were recalled to their posts and pagan subjects were granted complete religious liberty.

Frederick the Great of Prussia believed that nothing existing in nature could be annihilated. Shortly before his death, he said, "I may not be a king in my future life, so much the better."

Born in humble conditions, Napoleon Bonaparte rose to dominate empires and with a single word removed kings from their thrones. During those strange conditions into which he would sometimes pass, Napoleon would cry out to his Marshals: "I am Charlemagne. Do you know who I am? I am Charlemagne!" In a meeting with several dignitaries of the Roman Catholic Church, Napoleon repeated every three or four minutes: "Messieurs, you wish to treat me as if I were Louis le Debonnaire (that is, as

King Louis XVI). Do not confound the son with the father. You see in me Charlemagne…I am Charlemagne, I…yes, I am Charlemagne."

Interestingly, Charlemagne was crowned Emperor of a revived Roman Empire (later styled as Holy Roman Empire) by Pope Leo III on Christmas Day, 800 A.D. A thousand years later (1806), Napoleon established the Confederation of the Rhine, ending the Holy Roman Empire that July. That August Francis II dropped his title as Holy Roman Emperor, having assumed the title of Emperor of Austria in 1804.

The most infamous commander and contemporary of General Patton was Heinrich Himmler, who claimed to be the reincarnation of Emperor Henry I, known as the Fowler, supposedly because the messengers announcing his election as Emperor found him hawking. The first of the Saxony Emperors, Henry forced recognition of his authority among nobles, and cool to the Church, avoided ecclesiastical coronation.

Near the end of World War II in Europe, Himmler commanded an Army Group, but did not come in contact with Patton's Third Army. Like Henry I, Himmler achieved great power as Reichsfuhrer of the dreaded SS.

The author of Brigadoon, My Fair Lady and Camelot, Alan Jay Lerner, expressed the view that child prodigies must surely have lived before to have been so gifted.

During World War II, William Dudley Pelly in his publication Soulcraft, suggested that General MacArthur was a reincarnation of General Washington. In 1978, Manchester's biography of MacArthur was titled American Caesar. General Patton wrote in his poem "Through a Glass, Darkly" of being a soldier countless times and in the last stanza "forever in the end dying a soldier." Could Caesar, Washington, and MacArthur be one personality?

On December 4, 2012, the author added the following appendix to briefly illustrate the long and ancient history of reincarnation, which General George S. Patton, Jr. would have encountered.

APPENDIX C

A Brief History Of Reincarnation

To the eternal question as to what happens after death, philosophy, religion, revelation, and experience have provided three answers:

1. Death is final, the secular view;
2. Life resumes at some future period in heaven, the Christian view,
3. Life will return on earth, the reincarnation view.

The reincarnation view dispels the pessimistic first view and relieves God of the injustice of only "one time around" in the second view.

Reincarnation, metempsychosis, and transmigration are often assumed to mean the same thing. Specifically, transmigration is rebirth in a new human, animal, and even plant; metempsychosis is rebirth in a human or animal; and reincarnation is rebirth in a new body on the same level of the physical evolutionary scale.

A most compelling evidence for reincarnation is the 1994-documented story of Shanti Devi, a young Hindu girl who remembered her previous life in detail. After her death in 1925, as Lugdi Devi, she was reborn fifteen months later as Shanti Devi and as a child nine years old led her parents to her previous home, husband and son.

Reincarnation is a major tenet of Hinduism as the fall and redemption of man is a basic tenet of Christianity. The earliest writings on samsara or rebirth are found in the Upanishads, which minutely classify every stage of spiritual

14

advancement. The most beloved scripture in India (comparable to the Christian Gospels), is the Bhagavad Gita. The principal teaching concerning the eternal nature of the soul is found in chapter 2.

Plato's detailed and subtle discussion concerning reincarnation is found in its fullest accounts in The Republic, the Phaedrus, and the Phaedo. Neoplatonism, whose principle spokesperson was Platonius, influenced early Christianity regarding reincarnation.

Platonius (205-270 A.D.) wrote, "The soul goes through different forms of existence. Our present existence was created as a result of our actions in the past."

Clement of Alexandria (150-215 A.D.), a Christian Platonist, makes a very clear statement of preexistence in his Exhortation to the Heathen. In First Principles, Origen, a student of Clement of Alexandria, makes an unmistakable statement of reincarnation, "The soul has neither beginning nor end…"

All the gnostic sects took reincarnation seriously and were for a time, more numerous than any other Christian group.

In the sixth century, the Byzantine Emperor Justinian instigated a local synod in Constantinople, which condemned Origen's teaching of the preexistence of the soul. In 553 A.D., the Fifth Ecumenical Council (the Second Council of Constantinople), announced the anathemas (curses) against Origen, "If anyone asserts the fabulous preexistence of souls, and shall assert the monstrous restoration which follows from it: let him be anathema."

The episode in the Bible of the man born blind at birth seems to point to reincarnation. Jesus is asked who had sinned, the man or his parents, that he should be born blind. Since the man was born blind, when could he have sinned? The only reasonable answer is in some prenatal state. The question explicitly presupposes prenatal existence, and Jesus said nothing to dispel or correct the presupposition. This passage in the New Testament supports the contention that Jesus and his followers accepted or at least were aware of reincarnation.

Dr. Ian Stevenson spent numerous years studying hundreds of instances where children or adults seemed to remember a past life. He discovered that children started recounting memories of previous lives between the ages of 2 and 5, but seemed to have forgotten them by the age of 8 or 9. Gradually, Stevenson began to consider reincarnation as a 'third possibility" in character development, along with heredity and environmental influences.

Stevenson suggested that further investigation of apparent memories of former incarnations might well establish reincarnation as the most probable explanation of these experiences.

Doctor Quincy Howe, Jr. concludes in Reincarnation for the Christian, that the New Testament concerns itself with the Kingdom proclaimed by Jesus and very little with the prenatal or postmortem life of man, precluding any arguing a case for or against reincarnation. Christian doctrine and the trend of Biblical scholarship have gone against reincarnation and concerns itself with questions that shed little light on the subject. The convinced reincarnationist, however, may be encouraged to make an intriguing case for reincarnation based on existing materials and research.

On December 4, 2012, the author added the following. A copy of a letter received from Major General George S. Patton, III, (Ret.) *to whom the author had forwarded a copy of the original booklet on his famous father.*

Major General George S. Patton
United States Army, Retired
650 Asbury Street
South Hamilton, MA 01982

September 13, 1991

Mr. Karl F. Hollenbach
Dunsinane Hill Farm
Ekron, Kentucky 40117

Dear Mr. Hollenbach:

Many, many thanks for your note and booklet on my dad.

Although I have scanned it at this time, I do look forward to reading it in more detail. You were most thoughtful.

Since we do hold most of the Patton memorabilia and papers at Ft. Knox, would you please consider sending a copy to:

Curator
Patton Museum
HQ USAARMC
Ft. Knox, KY 40121

They might consider marketing it for you at the little store. If not, a copy should go to the library which is in the Museum proper.

Again, my thanks.

Faithfully,

George S. Patton
Major General, US Army (Ret)

GSP:lh

17

BIBLIOGRAPHY

Ayer, Frederic, Jr. *Before the Colors Fade, Portrait of a Soldier: General George S. Patton, Jr.* Boston: Houghton-Mifflin Co., 1964.

Blumenson, Martin. *The Patton Papers, 1885-1940, Volume* 1. Boston: Houghton-Mifflin Co., 1972.

___ ,. *The Patton Papers, 1940-1945, Volume II*, Boston: Houghton-Mifflin Co., 1972.

Essame H. Patton: *A Study in Command.* New York: Charles Scribner's Sons, 1974.

Farago, Ladislas. *The Last Days of Patton.* New York; McGraw-Hill, 1981.

_____. *Patton Ordeal and Triumph.* New York; Van Obolensky, 1963.

Gaynor, Frank, Ed., *Dictionary of Mysticism.* New York. 1953.

Head, Joseph and Cranston, S.L., Ed., *Reincarnation: An East-West Anthology.* Wheaton, IL. A Quest Book, 1968

Hogg, Ian V. *The Biography of George S. Patton.* Greenwich, CT; Bison Books, 1982.

Howe, Quincy, Jr., *Reincarnation for the Christian.* Philadelphia. The Westminster Press, 1974

Langer, William L., Ed., *An Encyclopedia of World History.* Boston. Houghton Mifflin Co. 1948

Lonnerstrand, Sture, *I Have Lived Before.* Huntsville AR. Ozark Mountain Publishers. 1994.

Patton, George S., Jr. *War As I Knew It.* Annotated by Paul D. Harkens. Boston: Houghton-Mifflin Co., 1947.

ABOUT THE AUTHOR

Karl F. Hollenbach was born in 1925 in Louisville, Kentucky. He received his B.A. and M. Ed. from the University of Louisville. His esoteric and metaphysical articles have been published in Japan and England as well as the United States. He and his artist wife live on Dunsinane Hill Farm near Fort Knox, Kentucky.

Additional information about the author may be found at http://BooksAuthorsAndArtists.com and on the Books, Authors and Artists Facebook page at https://www.facebook.com/BooksAuthorsAndArtists

by Karl F. Hollenbach

ANECDOTES AND SPECIAL NOTES
    Amazon Kindle ebook: http://amzn.to/16pgHtU
    Amazon paperback: http://amzn.to/10Dmb1v
    CreateSpace paperback: https://www.createspace.com/4278307

FRANCIS ROSICROSS
    Amazon Kindle ebook: http://amzn.to/1klGlGu
    Amazon paperback: http://amzn.to/1d3pzIi
    CreateSpace paperback: https://www.createspace.com/4521941

HANDBOOK – APPLYING METAPHYSICAL
PRINCIPLES IN TEACHING
    Amazon Kindle ebook: http://amzn.to/Ysuo3o
    Amazon paperback: http://amzn.to/Y1O6Df
    CreateSpace paperback: https://www.createspace.com/4035946

THE GREAT HAWK
    Amazon Kindle ebook: http://amzn.to/Z9TCo5
    Amazon paperback: http://amzn.to/1513XGb

CreateSpace paperback: https://www.createspace.com/4044068

HOLY GROUND
Amazon Kindle ebook: http://amzn.to/1lTsnv2
Amazon paperback: http://amzn.to/1fLaHkS
CreateSpace paperback: https://www.createspace.com/4727103

A JOURNEY TO THE FOUR KINGDOMS
Amazon Kindle ebook: http://amzn.to/YCQpwJ
Amazon paperback: http://amzn.to/15l16Ig
CreateSpace paperback: https://www.createspace.com/4136583

MANSIONS OF THE MOON (formerly ERICIUS)
Amazon Kindle ebook: http://amzn.to/1gYq8p6
Amazon paperback: http://amzn.to/1f8r2yy
CreateSpace paperback: https://www.createspace.com/4428046

PATTON: MANY LIVES, MANY BATTLES
Amazon Kindle ebook: http://amzn.to/XIjvsm
Amazon paperback: http://amzn.to/WFENtl
CreateSpace paperback: https://www.createspace.com/4097702

THE RIGHTEOUS ROGUE
Amazon Kindle ebook: http://amzn.to/12QAMWD
Amazon paperback: http://amzn.to/13CHeiD
CreateSpace paperback: https://www.createspace.com/4247817

SCROOGE AND MARLEY
Amazon Kindle ebook: http://amzn.to/XWgQPs
Amazon paperback: http://amzn.to/WFEoXJ
CreateSpace paperback: https://www.createspace.com/4055049

THRICE TOLD TALES
Amazon Kindle ebook: http://amzn.to/17YzgH5
Amazon paperback: http://amzn.to/14wpXZV
CreateSpace paperback: https://www.createspace.com/4280447

THRICE TOLD TALES: LARGE PRINT EDITION
Amazon Kindle ebook: http://amzn.to/1jBITzW
Amazon paperback: http://amzn.to/1eblTEg
CreateSpace paperback: https://www.createspace.com/4614310

How to Contact Karl F.:

Goodreads:
http://www.goodreads.com/search?utf8=%E2%9C%93&q=Karl+F
.+Hollenbach&search_type=books

Publisher's Facebook:
https://www.facebook.com/BooksAuthorsAndArtists

Amazon's Author's Page:
http://www.amazon.com/Karl-F.-
Hollenbach/e/B00B36VS38/ref=sr_tc_2_0?qid=1363387919&sr=1-2-ent

Where to purchase books by Karl F. Hollenbach:

Please see the Amazon and CreateSpace links under each title above.

YOUR REVIEW IS IMPORTANT!

We appreciate your support for Karl F.

In advance, we are very grateful for your review of any of his works. Please post a review, with your analysis, thoughts, and ideas at:

Amazon: http://amzn.to/XIjvsm
Goodreads:
http://www.goodreads.com/search?utf8=%E2%9C%93&q=Karl+F.+Hol
lenbach&search_type=books

Karl F. Hollenbach, as author, interviews Mr. James Autenrith, organist at General Patton's funeral.

AUTHOR: Mr. Autenrith, how did you come to be the organist at General Patton's funeral service?

AUTENRITH: I joined the Enlisted Reserve Corps in October 1942, while a sophomore student at the State Teachers College, in Potsdam, New York. I was called to active duty in the spring of 1943 and was selected for the A.S.T.P engineering course at the University of Alabama.

AUTHOR: That was the Army Specialized Training Program?

AUTENRITH: Yes. I took infantry basic training and then entered the University, but the program ended shortly after that and I was assigned to the ill-fated 106th Infantry Division.

AUTHOR: Wasn't that the division first attacked by the Germans during the Battle of the Bulge?

AUTENRITH: Yes, it was. The division was deployed along a rocky, wooden ridge when the Germans began an artillery barrage while English speaking, German soldiers, wearing captured American MP uniforms, added to the confusion.

AUTHOR: M.P.? That's Military Police?

AUTENRITH: Yes. The division lost 7,000 men and 1,000 dead or missing. I was with the 106th Division only a short time before being assigned to and going overseas with the 147lst Engineer Maintenance Company in January 1945. I served in France and Germany with General Patch's Seventh Army, and then after V-J Day...

AUTHOR: That would be Victory - Japan ... the end of the War in the East.

AUTENRITH: Yes. The European war ended in May of 1945 and three months later, the Pacific war ended. After V-J Day, I transferred to the 504th Quartermaster Battalion Headquarters as a chaplain's assistant. The battalion was sent to Neckarstadt, a suburb of Mannheim, Germany, which was just a few blocks from where General Patton's accident occurred.

I was in charge of a central chaplain's bureau, scheduling church services for a number of Army units in the area, and playing for Army church services on a famous four-manual organ in the Christ Church (the Christus Kirche).

AUTHOR: That was more your profession.

AUTENRITH: Very much so. I was able to study at the Army's I and E School...

AUTHOR: Information and Education School?

AUTENRITH: Yes. That was in Heidelberg University.

AUTHOR: I understand that Heidelberg was not bombed.

AUTENRITH: That's true. Apparently, there was an informal understanding that the Allies would not bomb the university town of Heidelberg and the German's would not bomb the university town of Cambridge.

At the I and E School I was able to take piano and organ lesson for several months and also became accompanist for the Seventh Army Chorus.

AUTHOR: General Patton had been authorized to proceed to the States around December 14th, I believe.

AUTENRITH: Yes. After spending Christmas with his family, I understood he intended to retire.

AUTHOR: He had been home a short time right after the war ended, before returning to Europe.

AUTENRITH: That's right. On December 19th, a day before he planned to return to the States, I understand, he went hunting pheasant with several of his staff. Near Mannheim, his Cadillac limousine collided with an Army 2-1/2 ton truck and the General was injured with a broken neck and taken to the hospital at Seventh Army headquarters in Heidelberg.

AUTHOR: That Cadillac has been restored and is in the Patton Museum at Fort Knox, Kentucky.

AUTENRITH: Yes, I've seen it and the special truck designed as an office and sleeping quarters for the General in his push through France across the Rhine into Germany along with a great deal more Patton memorabilia.

At the time of the accident, I was travelling from Mannheim to Heidelberg every day, rehearsing with the Seventh Army Chorus and the Heidelberg Symphony Orchestra in preparation for a Christmas Eve broadcast of Part I of Handel's "Messiah," which was to be heard around the world on the Armed Forces Network. Since my duties as a chaplain's assistant included playing the organ for church services, and I was performing as organ accompanist with the Army Chorus, I was selected to play the organ at the church funeral on December 23rd.

AUTHOR: Wasn't Mrs. Patton there for the funeral?

AUTENRITH: Mrs. Patton had flown to Germany with Dr. Sperling, an outstanding brain surgeon from Louisville, who was ordered to attend to General Patton. Mrs. Patton was a guest in the palatial residence of General Keyes, Seventh Army commander, on the Schloss-Strasses near the old castle overlooking the city of Heidelberg. Near the Keyes residence was another mansion, the Villa Reiner, which was used as a VIP guesthouse, and the body of General Patton laid in state there for two days prior to the funeral.

Hundreds of officers, enlisted men, and dignitaries from other countries came to the Villa to pay their respects and to sign the memorial book.

On a landing on the stairway leading to the second floor, was a small pipe organ, and on December 22nd, the day before the funeral, another chaplain's assistant and I were assigned to play soft organ music during the day and part of the night, as visitors came and went downstairs.

We took turns playing so each of us could have a rest period. Mrs. Patton occasionally sent a note requesting favorite hymns be played.

Christ Church is located some distance from the crowded "down-town" area of Heidelberg and was a good location for the reception of dignitaries at the church and for the organization of the march to the central railroad station a few blocks away following the funeral service on December 23rd.

The Seventh Army Chaplain and Col. Edwin Carter, the senior Episcopalian in the U.S. Forces, European Theater, conducted the funeral service. I had been instructed to play organ music for one-half hour preceding the service. Since I had very little organ music with me in Germany, I was able to borrow music that I wanted to play from Dr. Oscar Deffner, the organist of Christ Church in Mannheim, where I played for military services every Sunday evening. Mrs. Patton had also requested a few favorite hymns. The actual service was very "Low-Church" with no communion, and followed a typical Army non-denominational format.

A large Army chorus from the Munich area sang one of Patton's favorite hymns, "The Son of God Goes Forth to War" and the Easter hymn, "The Strife is O'er," and two of his favorite Psalms were included in the service.

For the Recessional, Mrs. Patton had requested Handel's "Largo" from "Xerxes," followed by other organ hymns, while the congregation left the church and the funeral cortege started for the train trip to Luxembourg, where the General was buried the next day.

The honor guard consisted of men from several Army divisions, with the divisional bands and all the ceremonial trappings of a formal military funeral parade.

AUTHOR: What about church decorations for the funeral service?

AUTENRITH: Since it was just two days before Christmas, the church was already decorated with Christmas wreaths and candles. This setting seemed appropriate for the funeral of an old warrior, and most of the church decorations remained in place.

General McNarney, the acting Theater Commander, headed the official delegation and honorary pallbearers. Generals Eisenhower, Bradley, and many other general officers had already returned to the States.

In a half-track, Patton was carried to a special funeral train where seventeen guns saluted him before the train doors were closed and taps blown. That night the train eased into the city of Luxembourg and the cortege marched to an American cemetery, followed by citizens of Luxembourg.

AUTHOR: Mrs. Patton broke her neck during horseback riding and was cremated. Is she buried beside the General?

AUTENRITH: No one can be buried with a soldier, not even a spouse. However, Frederic Ayer, Patton's nephew, stated that he believed Patton's family scattered Mrs. Patton's ashes privately by her husband's grave.

Lieutenant General Geoffrey Keyes, commander of the Seventh Army, and on behalf of Mrs. Patton, sent me a personal letter of appreciation for playing in the Memorial Services. I appreciated his closing lines that the "rendition of the music was superb."

AUTHOR: Did you keep the letter?

AUTENRITH: Assuredly. I've left my account of the Patton funeral with the Patton Museum at Fort Knox and the Army Military History Institute, Carlisle Barracks.

AUTHOR: Would you play something for me?

AUTENRITH: I'd be delighted!

###

Made in the USA
Las Vegas, NV
07 April 2021